SUPERFOODS
INDEX

Top 50 foods to boost health and vitality

SEANA SMITH

First published by
Jane Curry Publishing 2013
[Wentworth Concepts Pty Ltd]
PO Box 780 Edgecliff NSW 2027 Australia
www.janecurrypublishing.com.au

National Library of Australia Cataloguing-in-Publication entry

Author: Smith, Seana.

Title: Superfoods index: Top 50 foods to boost health and vitality / Seana Smith.

ISBN: 978-0-9872275-8-4 (print edition)
ISBN: 978-1-922190-12-3 (Epdf edition)
ISBN: 978-1-922190-13-0 (Epub edition)
ISBN: 978-1-922190-14-7 (Kindle edition)

Subjects: Natural foods.
Nutrition.
Antioxidants—Nutritional aspects.
Detoxification (Health).

Dewey Number: 641.302

Cover images: Getty Images, shutterstock
Cover and internal design: Deborah Parry
Production: Karen Young
Printed in Australia by McPherson's Printing Group

Table of Contents

Are you ready to supercharge your diet? Ready to cast aside the foods that are not doing your body and brain any favours? Ready to choose widely from this list of the top 50 superfoods and ramp up the nutrition in your food and drink choices?

It's easy!

So what is a superfood?

Some foods are simply more nutritious, better for you, **more packed with the good stuff**. These are the superfoods. And if we all ate more of those foods, we'd be healthier, happier and, very probably, wealthier and wiser too.

Healthier because our bodies absolutely need protein, minerals, vitamins, good carbohydrates and fats, antioxidants and much, much more to function optimally.

Happier because the brain needs all that good stuff too, especially the good fats and vitamins.

Wealthier because we won't be spending heaps of money on either:

- Bulk junk food that leaves you literally starving for vitamins and minerals, locked into a cycle of overeating to try to give your body what it craves and needs.
- Bottles of expensive supplements; it's well known that generally our bodies absorb far more nutrients from real, whole foods than from anything in a capsule.

Wiser because of that better functioning brain and because we all know for sure that over-processed foods and junk foods dull the mind, as well as the body!

It's about quality AND quantity

It's all very well knowing that cloves have the highest amount of excellent polyphenolic antioxidants, and by a huge margin. But unless you are going to eat 100 grams at a time, are they really that useful? Have you ever tried to eat 100 grams of cloves??!!

It's better to know that drinking four to five cups of tea a day is also going to deliver a great antioxidant boost. Or perhaps to know that a daily diet featuring an **abundance of the fruit and vegetables** listed in this book will give you SO much more nutrition than the **odd expensive handful** of the next trendy so-called superfood to come along.

It's also important to understand that some fruits and vegetables are better than others, as are some meats, some nuts and even some drinks and sweet treats.

Isn't superfood a term just used and abused by marketers?

Well, the term does get abused a bit these days. If you see the word 'superfood' used in the same sentence as multi-level marketing, it's probably a good idea to run away screaming.

But seriously, in every food group there are simply some foods that are SO much more nutritious, SO much better for you. Very often these have been used both as powerful foods and also medicines for thousands of years. Modern medical research has at last been catching up with the wisdom of the ages to explain why these foods really are superfoods.

For example, when you think of fruits, which ones stand out as the best for you? Believe me it's not an apple a day that will keep the doctor away.

Think blueberries and raspberries or the mighty blackcurrant or elderberry instead. And don't just sprinkle them on your porridge! Get into the habit of eating 100 grams a day, or make it even more. That's the way to really pump up your diet. Find the good stuff in every food group and set it squarely in the middle of your plate, bowl or cup.

Superfoods for weight loss

There's a move afoot to concentrate less on what foods we shouldn't eat, and to look more at foods we can happily eat more of. Good plan! Eating nutrient rich foods fills the body up, lets the body know that there is plenty of what it needs and helps stop cravings for unhealthy junk.

Too many people are overweight yet undernourished. There are serious concerns in the medical community about the levels of fibre, vitamins D, A, C and E as well as calcium and potassium in the average diet.

Eat nutrient rich foods and you won't have to worry about being undernourished. Eat whole nutrient rich foods and you'll find that they can give you everything your body and brain require and for FAR LESS CALORIES than nutrient-poor foods.

Don't just count calories, make your calories count more!

PS Don't forget to move that body too, wiggle, jiggle, dance, hop, skip, jump or jog. Your heart deserves it and your brain will thank you for a bit of movement too!

Variety is the spice of life

Don't forget it's really vital to **eat a wide variety of superfoods as well as a wide variety of foods in general**. That's why I've included more information than just the top 50. Read through the 'Best of the Rest' sections and eat plenty of these foods too.

Your body and brain will benefit from **diversity**, from indulging in the thousands of nutrients that foods contain. So eat lots and lots of different fruits, vegetables, nuts, meat, fish, lentils, beans, spices, herbs and drinks.

Different foods contain different amounts of vitamins and minerals as well as the thousands of phytochemicals and antioxidants that we know are vital for optimum health. It's a simple equation: eating a wide variety of foods will give you a wide variety of nutrients. Your body needs them!

Your body deserves the best and so does your brain.

So let's celebrate the food that is really good for us.

And let's eat plenty of it!

Top 50
Superfoods

Acai, Goji and Inca Berries

This trio of superberries have become in many ways the poster boys and girls for superfoods. There's no doubt that all of them are rich in some great nutrients, they have excellent antioxidant levels and other health benefits too. However, they do cost a lot more than other fruits and berries! You can get more nutrient bang for your buck by eating larger quantities of other, much cheaper, berries, fruits and veggies. But if you're looking for some new tastes then why not try these berries, they are delicious as well as nutritious.

- inca berries are a really terrific source of fibre, 19% fibre by weight and mostly insoluble fibre — terrific
- goji is a good protein source with 12% protein, compared with 20% protein found in beef
- all of these berries are a terrific source of antioxidants
- all of these berries are high in vitamin C
- all three have high levels of some trace minerals, particularly inca berries which are high in potassium and phosphorus

Sprinkle dried berries on top of cereal or soak then add to breakfast smoothies

Add to mixed nuts for a terrific mid-meal snack

Use instead of apricots and other dried fruits in curries and other savoury dishes

Almonds

Yes, all nuts have a high percentage of fat, but rest assured that most of the fat in nuts is good for you. Indeed the almond, that old faithful, has some of the highest levels of good fats amongst all of the nutritious nuts. Almonds are also densely packed with a fantastic variety of vitamins, minerals, protein and antioxidants, and they've even been proven to work well as part of a weight loss program. Go nuts!

- very high in monounsaturated fats
- full of fibre
- high in protein
- high in vitamins E and B2, as well as magnesium, potassium, iron and phosphorous
- good source of calcium
- 30mg of almonds daily has been shown to lower LDL cholesterol
- almonds help you feel fuller for longer, so are a good snack food
- nut consumers seem to excrete more fat than people who don't eat nuts

Buy as fresh as possible, and get into the habit of buying whole almonds with their skins on, for the fibre and extra antioxidants

Store in airtight containers, ideally in the fridge

Eat the skin too

Toast them yourself, it only takes a few minutes in a hot oven but the taste is sensational!

Asparagus

This slender stem has been used as both a food and a medicine since the time of the Ancient Egyptians. The Romans would eat it fresh in spring then dried throughout the winter. Don't let the very delicate flavour and colour of asparagus fool you, it's bursting with vitamins and minerals and deserves a place in every healthy kitchen. Usually seen in its green variety, you might also find white and even purple asparagus these days.

- very high in vitamin K
- very high in folate
- high in vitamins C, E and B
- high in the amino acid asparagine, named after the asparagus
- high in fibre
- high in a wide variety of antioxidants
- good source of zinc, iron, manganese and magnesium
- very low in calories

Buy as fresh as possible, the stalks should snap crisply and be moist and juicy

Store in the fridge, try upright in a jug of water like flowers or wrapped in a damp cloth and put into a plastic bag

Eat asparagus raw in salads

Cook it very quickly, it only needs a very light steam, blanch, fry or braise

Try asparagus soup, risotto, and in pastas and frittatas

Use asparagus as a hangover cure, research suggests it may help break down alcohol in the bloodstream

Avocado

This fantastic fruit is nutrient dense and filled with the good fats that our bodies and brains need. The luscious avocado is a food that will fill you up and help you feel great. Eating avocado in a colourful salad seems to increase the absorption of all the antioxidants in the other vegetables, probably due to the avocado's good fats.

- high in vitamins C, K and E
- rich in folate
- high in fibre — half an avocado has around 5g of fibre
- high in the carotenoid lutein, great for skin and eyes

Buy avocados that are blemish free, and don't worry if they are unripe, avocados never ripen on the tree, they only start to ripen once they are picked

Ripen your avocados at home — you can pop them in a paper bag with a banana or apple to speed up the process

Swap butter for avocado on your breakfast toast or lunchtime sandwiches

Make green smoothies with avocado, spinach, banana, mango, milk and yoghurt. Try it, you'll like it!

Blend avocado and chocolate to make nutritious and delicious desserts, you'll find great recipes online

Babies tend to love avocado, give them a great start in life by including it amongst their first foods

Barley

Don't think of this cereal crop as being most useful when made into beer. Barley is a splendid wholegrain food that is regaining popularity after being overshadowed by wheat and oats for far too long. Barley can be bought simply dehulled, also known as scotch or pot barley, and this is the most nutritious type. It is also commonly sold as pearl barley, meaning the barley has been dehulled then steamed and polished. Although some of the bran has been removed, pearl barley is still a terrific and nutritious grain.

- very high in fibre which can help reduce blood cholesterol levels as well as being good for the gut flora
- very high in selenium
- high in copper, manganese and phosphorus
- high in the essential B vitamins

Enjoy boiled or steamed barley in place of rice, potatoes or couscous, the slightly nutty flavour and pleasant chewy texture might surprise you — use three parts water to one part barley and simmer

Make barley risottos, a welcome change from the usual rice

Add to soups and stews to boost fibre and add nutrients, flavour and texture.

Substitute barley flour for 25% of the wheat flour in cakes, biscuits and breads

Beans and Lentils

Raise a cheer for the loveliness of legumes and the pulchritude of pulses. Or you can just give a cheer for beans and lentils if you prefer. Loved for their taste and texture, for their versatility and for their very solid nutritional credentials, beans and lentils are a must-cook both for vegetarians and omnivores.

- very low GI source of carbohydrate
- useful amount of protein that is very easily digested
- terrific source of soluble fibre, plus amylose, a prebiotic resistant starch which is good for the gut
- good source of iron, magnesium, phosphorus and zinc
- rich in antioxidants

Buy them in cans for a simple life

Buy beans dry then soak and boil them for a much cheaper if more fiddly alternative

Rinse off the liquid to reduce the salt content of canned beans and lentils

Swap potatoes and rice for dhal or mashed beans, equally as filling but much more nutritious

Vegetarians love their beans and lentils and quickly become expert legume and pulse cooks

Don't miss out if you're an omnivore, add beans or lentils to your stews, soups or bolognaise sauces and enjoy the taste and extra phytochemicals

Blueberries

Small and round, sweet and tasty, the diminutive blueberry punches well above its weight nutritionally. Just 100 grams of the mini fruit contains as many antioxidants as two and a half cups of spinach! Buying blueberries doesn't have to break the bank either. Frozen blueberries are always in season and not too costly given the nutritional benefits.

- rated number one of all fruit and vegetables for antioxidant activity
- scientific studies show blueberries can improve memory and motor skills amongst the ageing
- high in vitamin C, B vitamins, beta-carotene and vitamin E
- high in fibre, very low in sugars
- high in the antioxidant anthocyanins which can improve heart and circulatory health and also eyesight, plus anthocyanins can help the body attack urinary tract infections
- contains resveratrol which protects the heart and pterostilbene which has anti-cancer effects

Buy fresh or frozen

Store in the fridge in a container, do not wash before storing — they can last for up to two weeks in the fridge

Drink as part of a brain and body boosting smoothie

Eat by the handful, for pudding with yoghurt, cream or ice cream, in fruit salads, with porridge, or in muffins

Add to salads. Yes, try it!

For kids they are excellent as an easy and non-messy snack

Broccoli

Broccoli is the groovy green nutritional giant of the cabbage family, much more nutrient-packed than it's leafier cousins. The broccoli we eat is actually a large flower head. Flower power! Broccoli is chock full of antioxidants, several of which are known anti-cancer agents. Almost all of which have excruciatingly long and complicated names. Broccoli also has anti-inflammatory properties and aids the body's detoxification system. Now there's a new broccoli kid on the black, broccolini, a hybrid of broccoli and Chinese kale with long thin stalks and smaller heads but a similar nutrient profile.

- high in Vitamin C (one serve gives twice your daily requirement!)
- high in vitamin K, beta-carotene and B vitamins
- high in folate
- high in fibre so bulky and filling yet very low in calories

Kids often love broccoli, chop it into little trees and make a forest of broccoli for them

Eat raw, yes, it's great raw in salads or to dip into healthy dips — eat it raw and lose none of its cancer-fighting abilities

Store in a sealed bag or container in the fridge

The stalk — eat it! Put it in soups or steam, bake or boil with the heads

Grows easily in cool climates

Brown Rice

Is brown rice really a superfood? Well yes and no, to be honest. There are certainly other grains that might seem better at first glance. For example, bulger wheat hasn't made the Top 50, yet has a lower GI than brown rice. The tipping point is that brown rice is cheap and universally available, and has some terrific nutrients. But, crucially, the message is, when you eat rice, eat brown not white. It's so, so much better for you. Opt for lower GI brown rice and don't eat in huge portions to keep the overall GI load less.

- super high in manganese
- high in magnesium, phosphorus and selenium
- high in B vitamins
- source of fibre

Choose long grain brown rice as it has a much lower GI than short grain

Store in an airtight container in a cool, dry place

Steaming rather than boiling also makes the GI of rice lower

Use one part brown rice to two parts water

Start your children off on brown rice and they'll love it for life

Mix lentils into brown rice to make salads and hot dishes too

Serve chicken and fish on a bed of brown rice, quick, simple and totally delicious

Cabbage

Nobody said you had to look sexy to be a superfood. That's lucky for the humble cabbage which turns out to be not-so-humble when it comes to delivering vitamins and minerals, all packaged up with a terrific dose of antioxidants. Learn to unwrap the outer leaves of the more colourful members of the cabbage family and you'll find a storehouse of cancer-fighting nutrients within. Your typical pale green cabbage doesn't pack the punch that the red and deep green varieties do but it's still a useful vegetable.

- very high in vitamin C, more than an orange!
- very high in vitamin K
- useful source of B vitamins
- useful source of potassium, manganese, iron and magnesium
- very low in calories

Buy whole cabbages as cabbage starts to lose vitamin C as soon as it is cut

Store in a plastic bag in the fridge

Choose dark green Savoy cabbages or bright red cabbages

Don't boil the poor old cabbage to death — learn to cook cabbage well, steam it, braise it or lightly stir fry, and also enjoy cabbage raw.

Kids enjoy biting into chunks of fresh cabbage, munching it like an apple

Capsicum and Chilli

These foods pack a punch, and not just for the tastebuds. Both capsicum and the smaller, more fiery chilli are full of antioxidants and a range of vitamins and minerals. Chillies are in fact the more nutritious, but it can be hard to eat a large amount of them! Do try to up your intake though, get used to the burn and you'll set your metabolism on fire. Red, yellow, orange and purple capsicums are much easier to eat in large quantities so in the end you will get plenty of great nutrients from eating them.

- high in beta carotene
- high in fibre
- high in vitamins C and K, plus the B vitamins
- high in potassium, manganese and magnesium
- high in antioxidants
- chillies boost the metabolism

Buy chillies and capsicum with smooth, taut skins and even colour

Store in the fridge, or chop up and freeze for longer-term storage

Choose red chillies rather than green, they have more nutritional oomph

Make capsicum soups, ratatouille, stews or caramelise with onions

Be generous when you add chilli to stir fries, chilli con carne, soups, curries and stews

Add chilli to desserts! Try chilli chocolate brownies, choc-chilli ice cream and chilli lime mango

Chia

Relatively new on the western superfoods market and rather over-hyped by some, chia is nonetheless a terrific addition to a healthy diet. Chia is a seed, but is often described as being a wholegrain food as it contains all the parts of other grain, the bran, the germ and the endosperm. Generally sold whole, you can also find chia flour. Both the white and black varieties have a similar nutritional profile.

- very high in healthy omega-3 fatty acids
- low in carbohydrate
- very high in fibre, 37% of chia is fibre, so it's an easy way to boost your intake
- high in protein, and it is a complete protein, meaning chia contains all eight essential amino acids — unusual for a plant food
- high in calcium
- low GI, chia makes you feel full so it is excellent for those watching their portions and weight

Buy as seeds, ground seeds or just the bran

Eat dry, sprinkled over breakfast cereal

Eat wet — mix it though your berry smoothies

Add chia to many, many dishes to boost their omega-3 levels, think salads, burgers, pancakes, muesli bars, stews and soups

Mix chia seeds with water to form a gel and use it to replace eggs or oil in baking, replace some of your white flour with white chia seeds

Chicken and turkey

Don't take it for granted, the much-loved chicken really is a superfood. It is a fantastic source of protein, essential to almost every cell in the body. Chicken is low fat too, not that we don't need fat, but we don't need too, too much of it.

- very high in protein, skinless chicken breast is one of the best source of lean protein in the world
- high in selenium and phosphorus
- good source of vitamin B6, niacin, vitamin A and vitamin B12
- has least impact on the environment of all land-based animal protein foods
- good source of magnesium
- high in the amino acid tryptophan which helps regulate the appetite, and improves sleep and mood

Buy organic or free range chicken if you can afford it, the nutritional profile is similar to that of commercially produced chicken but the taste is better (and the chickens are happier and are not routinely fed antibiotics!)

Store plenty of chicken in the freezer, then you always have on hand the basics of a healthy meal

Before cooking, remove the skin — for most dishes you don't need it and it is very fatty

Cook thoroughly — cooks very quickly

Keep your own chickens, they are not difficult to raise and they do provide eggs

Citrus Fruits

Drop those apples right now and pick up some citrus fruits instead. Citrus is many times more powerful nutritionally and not just for its very high vitamin C levels. Grapefruits, oranges, lemons, limes, satsumas, mandarins, tangerines and tangelos, eat whichever you like or better still eat a good variety of all citrus fruits and you'll get a zing from the taste and the nutrients.

- very low GI
- high in soluble and insoluble fibre, especially the pith
- exceptionally high in vitamin C
- high in folate
- powerful antioxidants are found in the fruit and also in the skin, some of which are proven anti-cancer compounds

Buy by the boxful when in season, citrus can be a very cheap purchase

Don't think that drinking orange juice is doing you anything like as much good as eating the whole fruit, it isn't! Find a blender strong enough and whizz peeled whole fruit with water to make a much better orange juice

Zest the skin of citrus fruits and use it to flavour yoghurt, as well as in puddings, cakes and biscuits

Pink grapefruit is especially antioxidant-packed, its carotenoids impart the pink colour and it has lycopene too

Add citrus segments to salads, the flavour works well with greens like baby spinach and the vitamin C helps you absorb the iron

Kids love a chopped up orange in their lunch boxes

Cocoa and Dark Chocolate

The botanical name of cocoa is *Theobroma Cacoa* meaning 'food of the gods.' Strictly the cocoa bean is not a bean, it's a nut and like all nuts, must be enjoyed in moderation. Pure cocoa powder is of course the best, there's no sugar and no fat and you can use it in so many ways. But dark chocolate is also pretty good for you, in small quantities. Shhhh… don't tell… there are other foods which are more nutrient dense. Perhaps they should edge dark chocolate out of the Top 50, but we know we love chocolate and indulging can be good for us in moderation. So if you won't tell, I won't either!

- rich in antioxidants called polyphenols, these keep your blood flowing well, can decrease inflammation and fight cancer
- has B vitamins, potassium and calcium
- very energy dense, especially chocolate

Buy chocolate in smaller portions and share with the family

Eat the very best chocolate and enjoy it enormously — in moderation

Try whisking cocoa into low fat milk and warming it for a lovely bedtime drink

Mix a large spoonful of cocoa powder into a berry smoothie for an extra antioxidant hit

Add cocoa and protein powder to your breakfast porridge for a sensational start to the day

Coconut

Young, mature, green, white, brown and hairy, flesh, water, milk and cream, the coconut comes to us in many variations and each has its own nutritional strengths. The coconut is a bit of an overlooked food source and well worth having a good look at and incorporating into more meals and snacks. Coconut is undoubtedly high in saturated fat, and needs to be eaten in moderation. However, most of the fats in coconuts are medium-chained saturated fats which do not raise blood cholesterol levels.

- super high in fibre
- very high in manganese
- very high in lauric acid, which is a killer of viruses, bacteria and fungi and boosts the immune system
- high in selenium, copper and iron
- energy dense, a good source of calories for those who need to eat plenty of them

Buy fresh young coconuts and use the gel-like flesh for desserts and drinks

Use lots of coconut in your cakes and biscuits and for making fruit and nut truffles and chocolates

Coconut works well in many soups, try with beans, pumpkin, chicken or crab

Curries really benefit from adding coconut milk or cream, delicious!

Coffee

Yes, coffee! Drunk in moderation, coffee has many health-boosting properties. Just hold back on sugar and too much milk and you'll be drinking a steaming cup of tasty anti-ageing and anti-diabetes substances. Yet remember, this superfood comes with a health warning. It can have bad health effects if over-consumed. Stick to three coffees a day and don't drown it in milk or stifle it with sugar.

- super high in the antioxidant polyphenols, in fact it is the sixth highest per serve after several berries and globe artichokes
- high in caffeine which has a stimulating effect on the brain and boosts the metabolism
- studies indicate that drinking coffee significantly reduces the risk of disease in men, it also reduces the risk of Alzheimer's disease and dementia in both men and women
- studies indicate that coffee protects against diabetes
- coffee drinkers suffer less asthma, however for those with asthma it has only a very small treatment effect
- green coffee is heavily promoted as a weight loss tool, but there is little credible evidence for this so far

Buy ground coffee or roasted coffee beans or buy raw green beans and roast your own!

Don't store coffee in the fridge, it's too moist

Do store coffee in airtight containers in cool, dry, dark conditions

Dark green, leafy vegetables

Go green, go as dark green as you can, and enjoy feeling like a nutritional saint. Why is the old advice to 'eat your greens' proving still so true in the modern world? It's the phytochemicals. 'Phyto' means plant in Greek, so the term just means chemicals found in plants, but the thing is, the deeper a plant's colour the more phytochemicals it has. And we're probably only scratching the surface in understanding just how good for us these plant chemicals are.

Silverbeet, Swiss chard, kale, watercress, rocket, beetroot leaves, endive and Asian greens like bok choy are just chock full of great nutrition. And the great thing is, it isn't difficult to incorporate a lot of these leaves into your daily diet. Just say 'salad!'

- high in folate which is a cancer-fighter and all round good guy
- all leaves are low in fat and calories
- very high in vitamin K
- the iron and calcium in Asian greens is particularly well absorbed
- high in the carotenoid antioxidants which are so vital for eye health
- high in beta carotene which converts to vitamin A

Buy a lot of leafy greens and just add them into everything, salads, stews and casseroles

Eat as much as you can, a huge bowl of leaves has so few calories and such great health benefits, fill yourself up, knock yourself out!

Drizzle your salads with a good quality oil-based salad dressing as oil will help your body absorb the nutrients

Do eat leafy greens in preference to taking vitamin A in tablet form, natural is best

Learn to love green smoothies, your body will love you for it

Eggs

The egg is the pocket rocket of the food world. Eggs are low in calories but absolutely packed with essential nutrients. Eggs are quick and easy to cook, can be used in a huge variety of dishes eaten at any time of the day. And cakes! Eggs are a cheap source of protein and there's no need to worry too much about the cholesterol, eat eggs daily and enjoy them.

- very high in protein — egg protein is of particularly high quality and is very easily digested
- high in vitamin D providing 20% of the recommended daily amount (RDA)
- high in vitamin B12, selenium and choline plus antioxidants too

Buy organic or free range if you can, hens raised outdoors who graze on plants also have higher omega-3 fats in their eggs

Look for omega-3 eggs from hens fed a diet high in omega-3 fats

Store eggs in their cartons in the coolest part of the fridge, but take them out and use them at room temperature for soft boiling and baking

For breakfast eggs have no peer, fry, scramble, poach, boil or make eggy bread

Excellent as part of any weight loss strategy

Flaxseed

Also known as linseed, this deceptively demure and diminutive brown seed hides its light under a bushel. It's the richest plant source of alpha-linolenic acid from which our bodies make omega-3 oils. You need to know about this little seed, especially if you are a vegetarian. The terrific thing is that we only need a small amount every day to really boost our intake of good fats.

- very high in alpha-linolenic acid
- high in lignans which lower female oestrogen levels, easing symptoms of menopause
- very high in thiamine
- source of protein

Buy whole seeds or ground seeds, or even ground LSA which is a mixture of linseed, sunflower seeds and almonds

Grind your own flaxseed as you need it, easily done in a blender or coffee grinder

Toast whole or ground flaxseed — gives a lovely nutty flavour

Mix ground flaxseed into yoghurt and add some berries

Drink some ground flaxseed in your nutrition-packed morning fruit smoothie

Add to savoury dishes like stews, meatballs and casseroles

Don't forget to drink lots of water when you eat flaxseed, as it is high in soluble fibre and will absorb water in the digestive tract

Freekah

A warm welcome to the latest of the new ancient superfood grains. Freekah is roasted young green wheat, a food that was eaten for many thousands of years then fell out of favour. The younger grain has more protein, vitamins and minerals than the more mature grains. Freekah has a delicious nutty flavour, it might almost be described as smoky. Freekah is sold as a wholegrain, a cracked grain and as freekah flour. Try it!

- higher in protein than the other grains
- high in fibre, four times as much as brown rice, mostly insoluble
- a low GI food
- rich in calcium, iron, potassium and zinc
- rich in the antioxidants lutein and zeaxanthin, important for eye health
- good source of B vitamins, and vitamins E and C

Use freekah in place of rice, pasta and potatoes as a side dish — boil or steam with four to five parts water

Add freekah to burgers and soups or eat as a breakfast cereal

Use in salads and to make pilafs

Replace a portion of normal wheat flour with freekah flour for a nutrient boost in your breads, cakes and biscuits

Garlic

Garlic has been used as medicine for millennia and it would be silly to stop now. In fact, scientists are now finding and testing the compounds that are so active and healthful. Garlic, in fairly large quantities, for example two to four cloves a day, has been shown to lower 'bad' cholesterol and high blood pressure. It is also a proven anti-bacterial, anti-fungal and anti-viral agent. Use it lavishly!

- high in allicin, a sulphur compound which is known to lower cholesterol and prevent tumour growth in the gut
- allicin is even thought to boost the sex drive

Store garlic in a dry, dark place at room temperature, with good air circulation. Do not refrigerate unless you have minced the garlic and put it in an airtight container

Peel just before using as garlic's potency is reduced when it is exposed to sunlight

Eat raw, in salad dressing, or rubbed on toast or in dips. Many people simply cut a couple of cloves into pieces and swallow them with a glass of water. Medicinal!

Roast whole bulbs of garlic then squeeze the garlic out and use it in dips, sauces and salad dressings, or simply eat on toast

Globe Artichoke

Thistles aren't only eaten by donkeys, you know. The globe artichoke is in fact a thistle and has been a favourite in Mediterranean cuisine for many thousands of years. No, you don't eat the spikes! Nor do you eat the flowers. Rather, you eat the very large edible bud below the flowers. Famed as a medicinal plant, the globe artichoke is now known to stimulate liver function and to have compounds which can lower blood cholesterol.

- very high in antioxidants
- high in fibre — amongst the highest of any vegetable
- high in cynarin which increases the flow of bile thus aiding digestion
- high in copper
- high in folate and vitamins K and C
- good source of magnesium, potassium and manganese

Buy fresh if you can, choose artichokes that feel heavy and have tightly packed leaves

Boil or steam the artichokes, then eat them with your fingers

Peel off the outer leaves and nibble the fleshy edible bottom portion, dipped into butter or hollandaise sauce

Then remove the fuzzy 'choke' and enjoy the succulent and delicately flavoured heart

Mash artichokes with potatoes, use to top pizzas or add to a warm or cold salads

Guava

The top of the crop as far as vitamin C is concerned, guavas hold more than any other food. We need to eat more of them! Guavas can have white, pink, red or yellow pulp. The skin is generally very thick and must be peeled off. There are many varieties grown and each has its own unique scent and flavour, but they are equal in nutrition. The seeds are perfectly edible so eat them up with the rest of the flesh.

- super high in vitamin C, the highest of any fruit
- high in beta carotene
- high in the antioxidant lycopene and other antioxidants
- high in copper and manganese
- high in fibre
- low in calories

Buy fresh guava that is blemish free, a ripe fruit will give slightly like an avocado

Guava season tends to be spring and summer only, you can buy tinned guava at other times

Store ripe guavas in the fridge

Peel then slice or cube the guava, eat as it is or add to fruit salads

Make guava juice, serve guava with cheese, try guava ice creams and sorbets, or slice into your favourite green salad

Herbs

Do you eat enough fresh and dried herbs to get the terrific nutritional benefits they offer? With heaps of fresh herbs available in most supermarkets, it's easy to pack more into your daily diet. Use them in lavish quantities as part of a green salad and you will be doing your body, and your taste buds, a great flavour favour.

- high in antioxidants, very high!
- herbs are packed with vitamins and minerals
- using herbs to flavour foods means that less salt is needed, always a good thing
- some herbs used in salad dressings, eg marjoram, can increase the bioavailability of antioxidants in the rest of the salad

Store fresh herbs with snipped stems in a glass of water; basil and parsley prefer room temperature, coriander prefers the fridge

Freeze fresh herbs in a single layer inside plastic bags

Grow your own herbs, many are easy to grow and are as happy indoors as outdoors

Make your own pesto and use it abundantly, try using herbs other than basil to make pesto too

Learn how to make your own tabouli, it isn't hard and it packs a great nutritional punch

Kiwi

This furry little fruit, which is in fact strictly a large berry, has become a firm favourite around the world in a relatively short time. Kiwi tends to be especially beloved by young children. This is terrific for the kids as it's so good for them. With its mild flavour and attractive green or gold colour, it's easy to eat plenty of kiwi!

- super high in vitamin C, a single kiwi provides double the amount an adult needs daily
- very high in the carotenoid lutein, excellent for eye health
- high in many additional antioxidants, plus vitamins K and E
- high in folate and also potassium and copper
- high in fibre

Buy firm, plump fruit with unblemished skin

Ripen in a paper bag with a banana if necessary

Warning! Kiwi decompose fairly quickly once ripe, so keep in the fridge

Cut a kiwi in half and simply scoop out the flesh with a spoon, then scoff!

Try kiwi in smoothies, fruit salads, mixed with yoghurt or ice cream,

Use kiwi as a meat tenderiser, add it to fish curries or use in sauces for fish, flesh and fowl

Lean Pork

Sorry, you'll have to put down that bacon and the ham too. The healthiest meats from the pig are the completely unprocessed lean cuts. None of the rest of the porcine meat is top quality enough to be described as a superfood. But the lean cuts can be, they certainly can! Lean pork is as low in fat as skinless chicken breast.

- very good source of protein
- high in zinc, with some iron but not nearly as much as lean red meats or liver
- super high in thiamine, also known as vitamin B1, which is essential to normal brain and body function
- good source of niacin, vitamins B6 and B12, selenium, riboflavin, zinc and omega-3.

Buy the lean and trimmed cuts of pork: loin steak, fillet, rump, round, topside and silverside steak, loin roast, diced pork and pork strips

Cook over a medium heat and be wary of overcooking, lean pork is safe to eat without overcooking — enjoy pork at its succulent best with a hint of pink left in the middle

Substitute lean pork for lamb, beef or chicken in your favourite recipes, remember it's always good to eat a wide variety of different foods

Lean Red Meat

Lean red meat is a superfood that has stood the test of time, from the days of our distant forebears hunting on the plain of Africa, most human populations have been meat eaters. Your body needs protein, and lean red meat can provide it efficiently whilst adding in other vital, health-giving nutrients. Lean red meat includes beef, lamb, goat, and game meats like venison and kangaroo. Don't forget that the body cannot store protein in the way it can fat and carbohydrate, so it needs a good regular supply.

- very high in iron and zinc
- high in vitamin B12, essential for optimum brain function
- lean protein fills you up and takes a long time to digest, so terrific for those wishing to lose weight
- good source of vitamin A in a form that is optimal for use by the body

Buy organic if you can afford it

Look for pasture fed meats, there are more omega-3 fatty acids

Before cooking trim off any visible fat

Eat cooked in many different ways, pan fried, stewed, barbequed, you can even eat meat raw in dishes like steak tartare

Ideally adults should eat 100 grams of lean red meat up to four times a week

Liver

Now don't screw up your face like that, learn to love liver and you'll never worry about being anaemic again. And you'll be guaranteeing your body a great supply of many other essential nutrients too. Hunter-gatherers across the globe have prized the liver of their prey for millennia — with very good reason. The standout nutrient in liver is of course iron, with pork liver providing the highest amount. Remember this is heme iron, which is much more easily absorbed that iron from plant sources.

- super high in iron
- super high in A and B vitamins, especially B12
- very high in folate, zinc and selenium
- one of the rare natural sources of vitamin D

Cook quickly in thin slices, fry, griddle or grill, braise or stew

Feed to the family a little at a time, add a few spoonfuls of finely diced liver to bolognaise sauce, shepherd's pie and other meals where minced beef is being used

Idea! If you can't bring yourself to cook liver then make a habit of finding a cafe or restaurant that serves it and enjoy it there. Italian cuisine especially has several tasty ways of presenting liver

Mango

Renowned for its sweet perfume and unique flavour, the mango is known as the 'king of fruits' for many good reasons. Mangoes are nutrient rich and unlike some other foods, are very easy to eat in large quantities. Ask any child! Mangoes are also tremendously versatile, you can use them in so many sorts of meals, cakes, puddings and drinks as well as in their raw, and very delicious, form.

- very high in beta carotene, the precursor to vitamin A — a whole mango can provide more than three times the recommended daily amount (RDA) of vitamins A and C
- high in vitamins C and B6
- high in pre-biotic fibre which is excellent for the gut
- high in polyphenolic antioxidants known to be protective against some cancers
- high source of potassium
- source of copper

Buy mangoes in season, they taste so much better when super fresh

Use your nose to check if a mango is ripe, it has a distinctive tropical, fruity scent, is firm but not hard and has an unblemished skin

Store at room temperature until fully ripe and then in the fridge, but never in a plastic bag

Babies tend to love mango, making it great to use as a first food

Milk

Go on, splash out on a glass of milk. It's such an easy way to boost up a few key nutrients. Make the milk low fat and you'll be lapping up even more health-wise. Calcium is the mineral we all associate milk with and we know how important it is for bones and teeth. But calcium also plays an important role in the workings of nerves and muscles and in making sure blood can clot efficiently. Three serves of dairy foods per day can provide most of the calcium you need, and in its most bio-available form. There are plenty of other vital nutrients in milk too and these are very important for good brain functioning and immune function.

- very high in vitamins D and B12
- very high in calcium
- high in protein
- high in the B vitamin riboflavin, essential for growth and for healthy eyes and skin
- high in phosphorus, potassium, magnesium and selenium

Start the day with a low fat milk and fresh fruit smoothie

Use in baking, for muffins and cakes

Evaporated milk is delicious in creamy curries or poured over tinned fruit for a quick dessert

Add milk to your evening meals in white sauces and frittatas

Mushrooms

Regarded as a health food for millennia by the Chinese, the nutritional qualities of the many varieties of mushroom and their rich flavour are now far more fully appreciated in the west. Neither a plant nor an animal, mushrooms form a separate food group, the fungi, and have unique properties. The most common forms you will find are white button mushrooms, large white field mushrooms, brown mushrooms and portobello mushrooms.

- just 100mg a day of mushrooms has been shown to reduce the risk of breast and prostate cancer
- very low in calories
- mushrooms can stimulate the immune system
- good source of selenium, potassium, riboflavin, niacin and vitamin D
- provide bulk in the diet and help you feel full

Buy fresh, or pick wild ones if you are SURE you know which ones are edible

Store in the fridge, in the cling-wrapped packaging they came in or in brown paper bags

Cook roast button mushrooms whole in a hot oven, slice and stir fry, add to salads, stews and casseroles, mushrooms soups are also excellent

Eat mushrooms for breakfast, start your day the nutrition packed way

Enjoy the texture of mushrooms as much as the flavour

Oats

Of course the Scots have known it for centuries, oats really are the best of the best when it comes to cereals and carbohydrates. Oats are a slow-burn food, keeping you full for a long time and filling you up with a great range of nutrients in the process.

- very high in a soluble fibre called beta-glucan, which is why oats lower blood cholesterol
- high in E and B vitamins, potassium, calcium, iron, zinc and selenium
- a very low GI carbohydrate
- high in protein compared to other cereals
- contain unsaturated fats
- gluten free, or almost gluten free — this debate is unresolved

Store in an airtight container

Buy rolled oats, they are far superior to the instant oats now available

Eat porridge and oatcakes, look what they've done for the Scots!

Try porridge with salt and a little butter, or with brown sugar, and raspberries or pear and cinnamon

Use oatmeal, it's harder to find but it makes a smooth, creamy porridge

Make your own superfoods muesli with oats, nuts and a small amount of dried fruits, add in ground flaxseed, some spices and reap the nutritional benefits

Bake biscuits and flapjacks with oats, and use oats to make crumble toppings for fruit

Oysters

Don't faint, just breathe deeply and get your head around the idea of upping your oyster intake. Your body will thank you for it. This marvellous mollusc is the richest source of zinc of any food on the planet. Oysters are not just high in zinc, they are superfood super-high. But zinc is not the only nutrient this brilliant bivalve is rich in.

- one oyster has 10mg of zinc, while a dozen will give you about ten times your daily needs
- high in iron, magnesium, phosphorus, selenium, iodine and copper
- excellent source of vitamins D and B12
- low in calories and fat

Buy as fresh as possible

Store in the fridge but NOT in water

Serve on a bed of ice with lemon on the side

Eat raw, oh go on slurp them down, a bit of lemon, salt and pepper is all you need

Bake, smoke, boil, fry, roast, stew, steam or broil them too

Try tinned smoked oysters for a quick zinc hit

Drink oysters as a cocktail with bloody mary or tequila. Go on!

Do eat them to improve your love life. Oysters have amino acids that trigger increased levels of sex hormone, evidently

Passionfruit

Get some passion back into the kitchen with this lip-smackingly tasty fruit. The passionfruit is a nutrient-dense fruit which is used far too sparingly. Most often seen in its purple form, passionfruit can also be yellow, gold, red and the larger red Panama variety. They are all nutritionally equal.

- super high in soluble fibre, higher than any other fruit
- high in beta carotene, the precursor to vitamin A
- high in vitamin C
- good source of B vitamins and iron

Buy fruit that feels heavy for its size, with unwrinkled skin

Store at room temperature for two weeks or in the fridge for four weeks — store in a plastic bag to prevent the fruit drying out

Freeze the pulp, in ice cube trays or small containers

Don't just use passionfruit as a decoration for pavlovas or fruit salads, make it the main fruit in your dish

Do eat the fruit just as it is. Simply cut the passionfruit in half and eat the pulp and seeds with a spoon. Kids love it like this!

Whizz into smoothies for breakfast, blend with yoghurt and cream for dessert, make passionfruit curd and lash it liberally onto toast or stir into plain yoghurt

Grow your own passionfruit vine, it's surprisingly easy

Peas

Peas bestride two food groups, like the nutritional colossus they are. They are both vegetables and legumes. They have the higher protein content of beans and similar amounts of fibre, but peas are more digestible. Sugar snap and snow peas are the pods of the peas, and are definitely vegetables.

- high in vitamins C and K and the B vitamins
- high in manganese, magnesium, iron, zinc and potassium.
- high in soluble and insoluble fibre, excellent for the gut
- high in cancer-fighting antioxidants which are also excellent for eye health

Buy frozen, keep it simple! Frozen peas tend to be much cheaper than fresh — peas are frozen within a couple of hours of being picked so all the nutrients get frozen in fast

Cook frozen peas very quickly, it only takes three minutes

Lightly steam sugar snap and snow peas, or eat them raw, they are delicious this way especially in salads

Peas are so versatile, eat them as a simple vegetable or as the basis for soups and curries — add them to casseroles, salads and stir fries

Experiment with pea guacamole, mash peas with potatoes, add to pasta sauces, stews and casseroles

Pomegranates

The rich, ruby red colour of these succulent fruits signal that they are incredibly good for us. Like all deeply coloured fruit and vegetables, pomegranates are packed full of health-promoting and cancer-fighting antioxidants. Within its leathery skin, the pomegranate holds hundreds of juicy red 'arils' each with a small pip inside. The distinctive taste of the pomegranate lends itself to many dishes as well as to simply being eaten as it is. As they are generally only available in autumn, gorge yourselves on pomegranate when you can!

- super high in the protective antioxidants named polyphenols
- high in vitamin C and potassium
- high in fibre
- low in calories

Buy firm pomegranates that feel heavy and whose skin is taut

Store at room temperature for a few days or for two–three months when refrigerated in a plastic bag

Better to buy and eat the whole fruit than to simply drink bottled pomegranate juice

Savoury dishes get a real boost from adding pomegranate, use it in a stuffing for chicken, or in a sauce or glaze for red meats

Bake pomegranates into muffins and cakes, or try pomegranate compote

Make your own pomegranate juice by blending the arils and straining the juice

Quinoa

Like chia, quinoa is a seed which is treated as more of a grain. Both are from South America and have been cultivated there for many thousands of years. Quinoa was known as the 'mother of all grains.' Quinoa comes in grey, black and white varieties, white being the most common. It looks and behaves a bit like couscous but packs more of a nutritional punch. A gluten free food, quinoa is increasingly been recognised as a valuable food because of its overall nutritional richness. Perhaps not a surprise when you consider it comes from the same family as spinach.

- high in protein including lysine, an essential amino acid unusual in plant foods — in fact, it is a complete protein unlike most grains
- low GI
- high in iron, B vitamins and potassium
- high in fibre
- mineral dense, especially manganese, phosphorus and magnesium
- good source of antioxidants

Buy in bulk, go on it's good for you

Store in airtight containers, keeps longer in the fridge

Cook by boiling for approximately 15 minutes then fluff with a fork — use stock instead of water for extra taste

Great for breakfast, and as an alternative to potatoes, rice and couscous

Bake into cakes and biscuits

Raspberries

Sink your teeth into some ruby red raspberries and you'll enjoy not just the flavours but also the terrific health benefits of this sweet, luscious fruit.

- super high in fibre, 100g of raspberries has just over 6g of fibre compared to a slice of wholemeal bread which has only 2.5g or two Weetbix which have only 3.6g
- high levels of many antioxidants, including several which help the fight against inflammation cancer and ageing
- like blueberries, raspberries are very rich in the anthocyanins
- high in vitamins A, C, E and K plus the B vitamins
- good source of potassium, manganese, copper, iron and magnesium
- very low in calories

Buy fresh in season, or pick your own if there's a farm near you

Choose deep red, shiny fruit that look firm and plump

Store in the fridge, but not for long as raspberries spoil quickly

Buy frozen all year round, frozen berries are generally much cheaper than fresh but have all the same nutrients intact

Enjoy a couple of handfuls for breakfast with porridge or in smoothies, try in vegetable salads too

Pack homemade ice cream with raspberries, or mix lots of frozen raspberries with slightly thawed commercial ice cream

Salmon and Other Oily Fish

Known for millennia as a 'brain food' salmon and other oily fish really are nutritional powerhouses. Science has finally caught up with traditional wisdom to explain why the oils found in salmon can keep the brain and body healthy and working at best. Eat these fish twice weekly, they are quick and easy to cook and taste delicious. In most western countries the majority of the population do not eat nearly as much fish as is advisable. So grab your shopping basket, or a fishing line, and get some salmon today!

- one of the richest sources of omega-3 fats
- protein packed
- low in saturated fats
- rich in zinc
- high in iodine, potassium, vitamins A, B and D, copper, iron and selenium
- source of calcium

Buy very fresh, or frozen (for convenience), most salmon is farmed, but look out for wild salmon in shops too

Store in the fridge or freezer, but eat quickly

Eat at least twice a week, steam, BBQ, panfry, use in pies, frittatas, with pasta, in stir fries and in salads — eat hot or cold

Did you know? Salmon can jump up to two metres into the air when swimming upriver

Seafood — Molluscs and Crustaceans

Three cheers for the mighty molluscs and the cool crustaceans! Seafood is really good for us and we must not run the risk of forgetting how to cook these simple and delicious sea creatures. Mussels, cockles, clams, pipis, scallops, octopus, squid, lobster, crab, bugs and abalone, they are all superfoods because of their super high levels of nutrition. These animals are more nutritious than red meat, they have more protein, most have less fat and they have lots more minerals. Some types have more protein and less fat than even skinless chicken breast.

- super high in protein, low in fat overall with good amounts of omega-3 fatty acids
- very rich in iron and zinc — mussels and octopus have twice as much iron as beef!
- rich in magnesium, manganese, phosphorous, selenium, calcium and B vitamins
- low in calories
- cholesterol alert for squid, fish roe, shrimps and prawns only

Buy from a fishmonger with a high turnover, or buy frozen

Start your seafood cooking adventure with garlic prawns, simple and delicious, then take it from there

Try seafood chowder, then crab cakes, mussels in white wine, bouillabaisse, and on and yummily on!

Eat a wide variety of seafood to reap all the benefits of their differing nutrients

Sea Vegetables

Sea vegetable is simply the term used for seaweed which is being eaten as a vegetable. Many types of seaweed can be eaten, and although they can look very different, all seaweeds belong to the algae family. Coastal people from all over the world have always eaten seaweed, and for very good reason. The common edible types are *nori*, the sheets wrapped around sushi; *arame*, sold in string-like strips, *dulse*, a strong flavoured seaweed; *hijiki*, a mild, almost sweet seaweed; *kombu*, a type of kelp; and *wakame*, a tender, deep green seaweed. Much research is going on looking at the benefits of seaweeds for those needing to lose weight. It looks promising! Go on, try a little seaweed, and if you like it, eat a lot.

- kombu is very high in iodine and all seaweeds are rich in this vital nutrient
- high in B vitamins, plus vitamins C and E, and also folates
- high in magnesium, calcium and boron
- useful source of iron and phosphorus
- high in antioxidants

Find seaweed in Asian stores and in health food shops, usually sold dried

Add seaweeds to soups, stir fries and salads, and use them in and around homemade sushi

Spices

Researchers are beavering away in laboratories all over the world, proving the health benefits of spices. Chock full of powerful antioxidants and with many health giving properties, the science is catching up with what people throughout the world have believed for millennia. Many spices are also rich in minerals and vitamins, but since most of us eat only small amounts of spices, can they make a difference? The answer is yes, but it's still a great idea to up your spice intake in general.

- cinnamon, only half a teaspoon a day, can help keep blood sugars low
- ginger can reduce nausea, joint inflammation and ease pain
- turmeric reduces inflammation and can inhibit cancer growth
- garlic kills off viruses and bacteria

Cook more spicy curries, give your taste buds a treat

Add some turmeric and other spices to the water when you cook rice

Drink more chai tea, and you don't need to add sugar, the spices 'sweeten' the drink

Add more fresh ginger, garlic and chillies to your stir fries

Bake more cakes, biscuits and puddings with cinnamon, cardamom, nutmeg and ginger

Spinach

Take a bow you leafy green Queen of the superfoods. Spinach is so good for us, can't you just tell from the bright green colour of its leaves? Spinach may be green and leafy and look a bit weedy and insubstantial but it packs a Popeye-powerful punch when it comes to nutrition.

- high in iron, magnesium, calcium, manganese, zinc and potassium,
- high in vitamins A, C, B6, K and E
- full of fibre
- an antioxidant hit with lutein and beta-carotene and others which promote eye health
- very low in calories, so enjoy spinach by the barrowload

Buy fresh or frozen, both are equally nutritious

Grow your own, spinach is easy to grow even in cool climates

Store in the fridge in a plastic bag or sealed container, if you need to wash spinach, do so just before cooking

Eat in copious quantities in salads, with a healthy fat which helps to get all the goodness absorbed by the body

Drink in green smoothies, a cup of baby spinach in a green smoothie

Cook in frittatas, omelettes and stir fries

Add to curries, bolognaise sauce, lasagne, stews and casseroles

Sweet Potato

Like most vegetables, it's a case of the more colourful the better when it comes to this terrific tuber. So choose deep orange sweet potatoes and reap the health-giving benefits. Start the kids on sweet potatoes when they're young and steer them away from white potato crisps and chips.

- high in fibre
- high in vitamins A, C, and B6
- high in potassium and manganese
- lower GI than white potatoes, lowest when boiled rather than baked

Store in a cool, dark and well-ventilated place

Swap sweet potatoes for your regular white potatoes. Immediately!

Roast them whole or cut into cubes and toss with salt, pepper, olive oil and herbs or cinnamon

Bake them in foil and top with cottage cheese, mash them with a little butter, milk and nutmeg

Eat the skin of the sweet potato, it has great nutrients and fibre and is perfectly edible

Excellent in curries and in soups, try out a recipe using sweet potato in a cake too!

Kids tend to love sweet potato, make sweet potato chips by baking thin slices brushed with olive oil, bake for ten minutes, turn over and bake again

Tea — Black, Green and White

Hold the sugar and you have in your hands a warm cup of steaming antioxidants. The benefits of a good cup of tea are now widely recognised, and in tea's case it's all about quantity as well as quality. Tea may not have just as many antioxidants as some other foods, for example if you look at the polyphenols, a type of antioxidant, then cloves top the lot and tea has a lot less. But it's a lot more pleasant to drink a few cups of tea than it is to eat 100 grams of cloves. All types of tea come from the same plant, for black tea the leaves are crushed and fermented, for green they are dried then steamed, for white they are simply steamed.

- very rich in polyphenols which seek and destroy free radicals
- appears to be a cancer fighter
- tea drinkers suffer less heart disease and stroke and have less bad cholesterol
- tea has no calories yet boosts the metabolism to burn energy faster
- tea has both caffeine and theanine which stimulate the brain

All tea is good tea, green and black tea both appear equally beneficial

Stick to four to five cups of tea a day and you will not have to worry about over-consuming caffeine

Tomatoes

There's nothing humble about the tomato. This excellent fruit, yes fruit, is chock full of the antioxidants. It's a cancer killer, especially when cooked and as a paste it is super high in lycopene, a super duper antioxidant. The orange and yellow tomatoes are as good for you as the rich, deep red ones, it's just a different but equally powerful type of lycopene. Now available in a vast variety of shapes and sizes, keep tomatoes as a firm fixture in your daily diet and reap the health benefits.

- richest source of lycopene on the planet
- high in fibre
- high in vitamins C, K, E and B6
- rich in essential minerals
- famed as a terrific food for heart health
- very low in calories

Buy as fresh as possible and any varieties you like

Store at room temperature, put them in the fruit bowl

Don't forget tinned, dried, semi-dried, or as tomato paste

Grow easily in sunny positions in spring and summer

Kids tend to love tomatoes, especially the small cherry and grape varieties, make them a tomato skewer with beetroot and cucumber, or give them whole to eat like apples

Cook in almost every dish you care to mention, and don't forget to simply roast or fry them, ideal as a breakfast treat

Walnuts

The whole nut looks like the human skull and when you crack it open, the nut itself looks like a brain! They don't look like the human brain for nothing, walnuts are a terrific brain food. Walnuts are the nuts with the most long-chain polyunsaturated fats. And you only need a small serving a day to reap the benefits.

- help lower bad cholesterol and raise good cholesterol
- a 30g serve gives you 90% of the recommended daily intake of omega-3 fatty acids
- high in antioxidants especially polyphenolic compounds — scientists say twice as many antioxidants as other nuts
- high in vitamins B and D, and folic acid
- high in manganese, copper, potassium, calcium, iron, magnesium, zinc and selenium
- good source of fibre and protein

Buy as fresh as possible, from shops with a high turnover, or in sealed packs from the supermarket

Eat just 28g a day for a nutrient boost

Store in the fridge, and only chop them as needed

Use in salads, add small amounts to fruit smoothies, bake into bread, brownies and cakes

Try walnut sauces for chicken, walnut pesto, walnut hummus and maple candied walnuts

Tastiest when toasted in a hot oven for just a few minutes

Whitefish

Although salmon and the other oily fish usually hog the healthy-eating limelight, please do not underestimate the non-oily species of whitefish. Most governments are busy encouraging us to eat more fish and they mean ALL types of fish. Whitefish like barramundi, snapper, flathead, cod, whiting, haddock, sole, plaice and flounder are terrific sources of protein, are very low in saturated fats and rich in vitamins and minerals. Make the whitefish species a weekly feature on your menu plan and your body and brain will thank you for it.

- very high in protein
- high in niacin, vitamins B6 and B12, phosphorus and selenium
- low in fat

Choose fresh fish with bright red gills, bright, clear eyes, clean, shiny skin and a pleasant, briny smell

Or buy frozen — flash frozen and vacuum sealed is by the far the best

Store in the fridge, on top of crushed ice if possible

Wrap fish in wet newspaper or baking paper and bake in the oven

Stew it, whitefish make excellent fish stews, especially tasty if you add in some delicious seafood too

Fish pies topped with pastry or mashed potato are often popular with kids

Yoghurt

No, no, no, not the sugary confection that poses as yoghurt on many supermarket shelves. The health-giving yoghurt that can protect your body from all sorts of nasties is the most natural yoghurt you can get, the plain and deliciously creamy, delectable one. And go full fat for extra taste and yumminess, it won't kill you. It's the good bacteria that your body will benefit from. Good, natural yoghurt is teeming with mini microbes, or probiotics, that can really enhance your gut flora.

- high in protective microbes
- high in calcium, protein and B vitamins
- very easily digested by the body
- your body absorbs more nutrients from yoghurt than from an equivalent amount of milk
- yoghurts, and other low fat milk products are now proven as a useful part to play in weight loss

Buy the best natural pot set yoghurt, you deserve it

Make your own yoghurt, it is easy to do at home and you need never run out

Eat yoghurt daily to keep topping up the good bacteria in your digestive tract

Add your own fruit, jam, nuts, seeds, maple syrup and even a dash of sugar

Make healthy dips using yoghurt as a base

Cook with yoghurt, add to stews and curries, bake into cakes and biscuits

Best of
the Rest

Bread

Choose anything except plain white bread — anything!! Seriously, there are so many other great-tasting options, why bother with plain white?

Try instead:

- sourdough bread, much lower GI than plain white even the white sourdough
- rye and wholemeal sourdough are much more nutritious
- wholemeal bread, get all the nutrition from a grain of wheat, why wouldn't you
- dark rye bread, often known as pumpernickel, it's low GI and comes in handy small serves
- wholemeal pita breads and flat breads

Drinks

Water is a popular drink that has stood the test of time, refreshing and calorie free!

Herbal teas and tisanes

Smoothies made from low fat milk, yoghurt and superfood fruits, hold the ice cream!

Vegetable juices, freshly juiced is best, add in some ginger for extra zing

Cocoa made with real cocoa powder and low fat milk

Skim milk

Mixed fruit and vegetable juices, get the kids used to these first and then switch to vegetable only

Whole fruit juices, try blending whole fruit with ice and water in a powerful blender

Pure fruit juices, in moderation

Red wine — a glass a day will do the trick

Fruits

There are so many fruits in the top 50 superfoods, and these are the ones that stand tallest nutritionally. But there are few, scratch that, no fruits that aren't beneficial. Feel free to eat widely and eat well when it comes to fruits.

Those which are better for you include:

- apples
- apricots
- bananas
- cantaloupe/rockmelon
- cherries
- cranberries
- grapes
- honeydew melon
- lychees
- papaya
- peaches
- pears
- persimmons
- pineapples
- plums
- watermelon

Grains and Cereals

Eat:
- brown rice
- bulgur/cracked wheat
- corn flakes
- corn tortillas
- couscous
- enriched white bread
- multi-grain bread
- popcorn — plain
- wheat cereal
- whole wheat cereal
- whole wheat crackers
- whole wheat noodles

Avoid:
- processed white bread
- white rice

Nuts

All nuts are pretty good for us being a source of good fats and protein. Nuts also have fibre and will keep you feeling fuller for longer, plus they appear to boost serotonin levels. But exercise restraint, a handful a day is as many as you need.

Brazil Nuts
- super high in selenium, a single nut can give you your ideal daily dose

Cashews
- high in magnesium, having even more than almonds, also high in iron and zinc

Hazelnuts
- good source of iron and a group of antioxidants named proanthocyanidins, highest in fibre

Peanuts
- high in folate, peanuts are strictly a legume but we'll draw a veil over that for the moment

Pine nuts
- source of omega-6 fats, high in zinc, iron, folate and fibre

Pistachios
- excellent source of potassium, high in cholesterol-lowering plant sterols

Protein Sources

There are so many good sources of protein that you can be spoilt for choice! Just steer clear of meats with a high fat content.

Cheese — the lower fat varieties like ricotta and cottage cheese are best. Eat the higher fat cheeses in moderation

Fish — grilled, barbequed, smoked but not deep fried. Tuna is a good source of protein, tinned or fresh

Nuts — *see* Nuts opposite

Pork — all lean cuts

Seafood — prawns, shrimp, crab

Seeds — pumpkin or sunflower

Tofu

Turkey — all lean cuts

Vegetables

There's no real best of the rest with vegetables because they are ALL good for you. The main message here is to eat vegetables abundantly, in vast quantities, as many as you can manage. Your waistline will thank you for it. So will your intestines, the fibre in veggies is so good for the gut and for the beneficial gut microbes that live there.

Think vibrant colours, make a rainbow on your plate.

Eat vegetables raw as well as cooked, both ways have their benefits.

Boost Your Nutrient Intake

If you need **B vitamins**, sprinkle **wheatgerm** over your breakfast cereal or add it to your smoothies or baking, or eat some **beef liver**

If you need **vitamin C** eat **guavas** or **kiwis**

If you need **zinc** eat fresh or tinned, smoked **oysters**

If you need **iron** eat **liver, mussels, oysters** or **red meat**

If you need **fibre** eat **kiwi fruit, chia** and **flax seeds** and **raspberries**

If you need **vitamin B12** eat **oysters, clams, mussels, liver, fish, meat** and **eggs**

Websites

Websites

Superfoods General Websites

The standout here is the website of the Nutrient Rich Foods Coalition.

www.nutrientrichfoods.org

The Nutrient Rich Foods Coalition is a US-based partnership of scientists, health professionals, communication experts and agricultural organisations.

The Coalition aims to inform and inspire people to improve their diets by eating more nutrient dense foods, and by association, less nutritionally poor foods.

Their website contains information and downloadable items both for health professionals and for consumers.

You will find:
- a shopping list of nutrient rich foods
- a guide to nutrition labels
- information on portions
- advice on fitting in 'fun' foods
- recipes
- meal plans

Other Recommended Nutrition Websites

Foodwatch

www.foodwatch.com.au

Australian accredited nutritionist and dietician Catherine Saxelby provides a wealth of information on eating well. Her well-balanced, expert approach is very reliable, and her recipes are delicious. She is the author of several influential books.

Dr Joanna

www.drjoanna.com.au

Dr Joanna McMillan is an Australian nutritionist and dietician whose website is packed with ideas and advice on healthy eating. There are terrific healthy and delicious recipes and information about her books.

Great Superfoods Recipe Ideas

If you are looking for some fantastic recipes using whole superfoods, then why not start off with the farmers who grow the superfoods?

Most food types have associations of farmers, the industry peak body. The **websites of many of these peak bodies have some fantastic recipes**.

Now I'm not doing all the work for you here. You can easily find these examples, which are all from the USA, UK and Australia. But they'd be easy to find in your own country too, for all the superfoods that are grown locally.

Here are some to get you started:

Australian Almonds
www.australianalmonds.com.au
The website of the Australian Almond Growers Association.

California Almonds
www.almondboard.com
The website of the Almond Board of California.

Australian Asparagus
www.asparagus.com.au
The website of the Australian Asparagus Council

California Asparagus Commission
www.calasparagus.com
Did you know, 70% of the USA asparagus crop is grown in California.

Australian Avocados
www.avocado.org.au
The website of Avocados Australia, the peak industry body for the Australian avocado industry.

Barleyfoods
www.barleyfoods.org
The website of the National Barley Foods Council.

Briteggs

www.lioneggs.co.uk

Website of the British Egg Information Website.

Eggs As Easy As

www.eggsaseasyas.com.au

The consumer website for the Australian Egg Corporation.

American Egg Board

www.aeb.org

You'll find hundreds of recipes on this site.

Yes peas!

www.peas.org

The website of the British Growers Association.

California Walnuts

www.walnuts.org

The website of the California Walnut Commission, there are wonderful walnut recipes here.

Author Bio

Seana Smith was born and brought up in Scotland. She now lives in Sydney, Australia with her hungry husband and four ravenous and very active children.

Seana is the author and co-author of three previous books, all published by Jane Curry Publishing:

Sydney For Under Fives

The Australian Autism Handbook (1st edition)

Beyond The Baby Blues

Seana blogs at: Sydney, Kids, Food + Travel
www.seanasmith.com

Blog topics include: The best of Sydney for kids
Family-friendly recipes
Family Travel
Life balance and mental health